© Peanuts Worldwide LLC

All scripture taken from the HOLY BIBLE NEW INTERNATIONAL VERSION®. NIV®. Copyright 1973, 1978, 1984 by International Bible Society. Used by permission of Zondervan.

Published by Hallmark Gift Books,
a division of Hallmark Cards, Inc.,
Kansas City, MO 64141
Visit us on the Web at Hallmark.com.

All rights reserved. No part of this publication may be reproduced, transmitted, or stored in any form or by any means without the prior written permission of the publisher.

Editorial Director: Theresa Trinder
Editor: Kim Schworm Acosta
Art Director: Chris Opheim
Designer: Brian Pilachowski
Production Designer: Dan Horton

ISBN: 978-1-63059-827-3
BOK1066
Made in China
1217

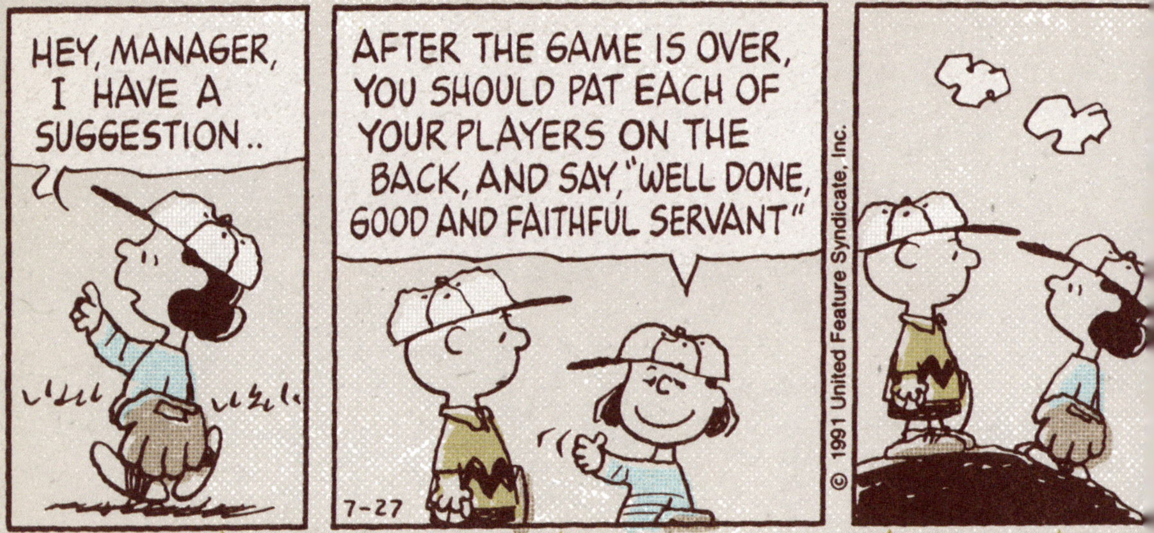

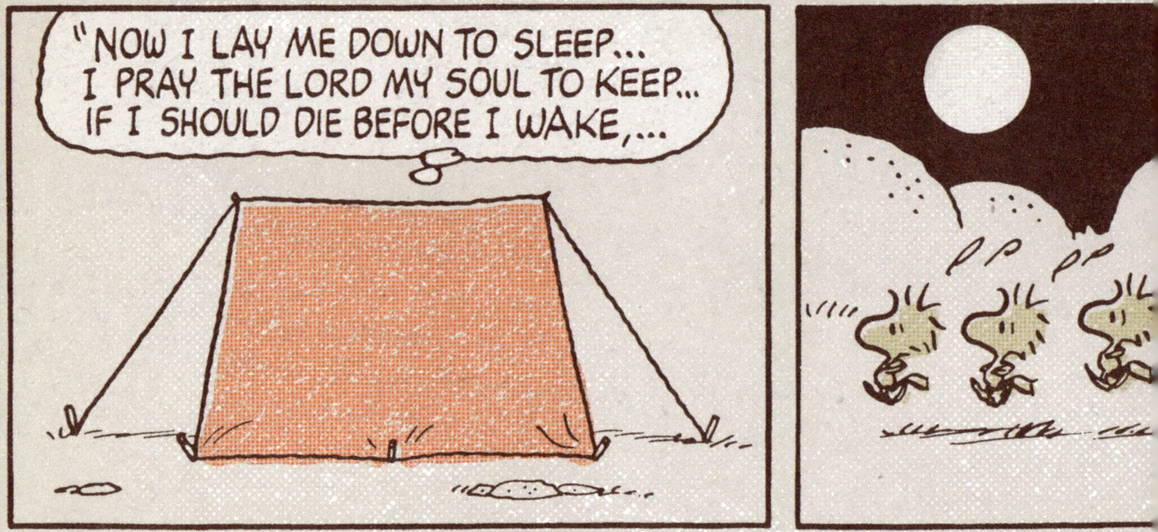

Our *mouths* were filled with *laughter.*

PSALM 126:2

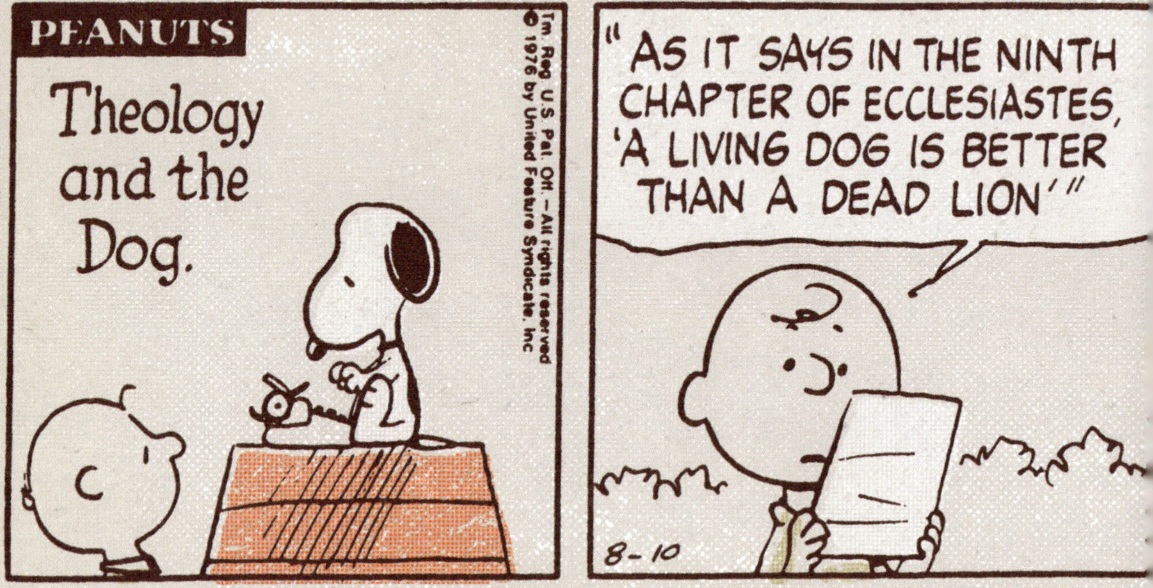

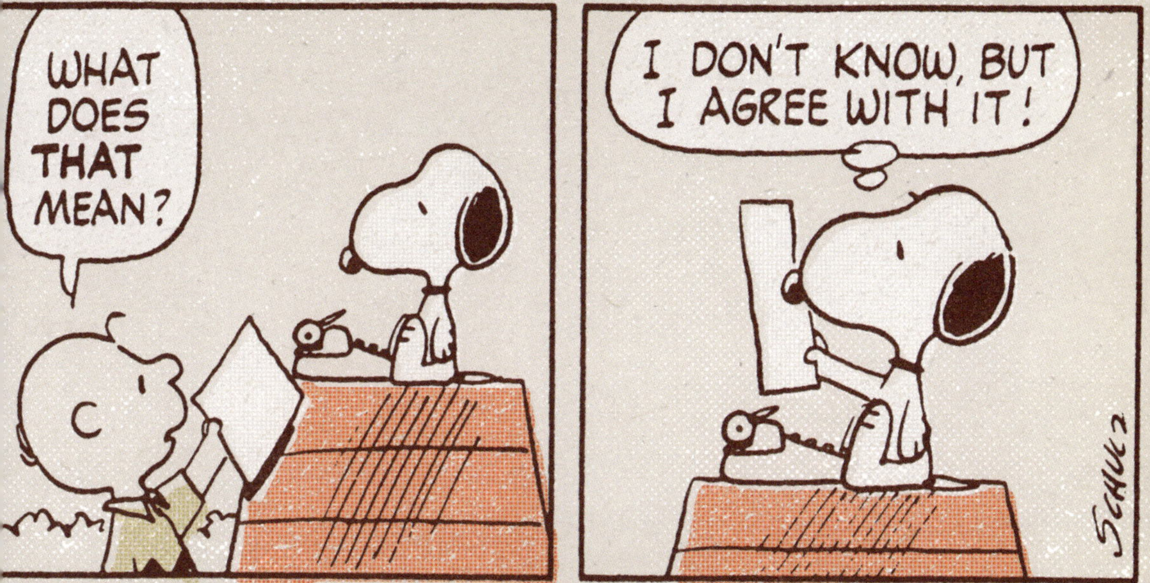
WHAT DOES THAT MEAN?
I DON'T KNOW, BUT I AGREE WITH IT!
SCHULZ

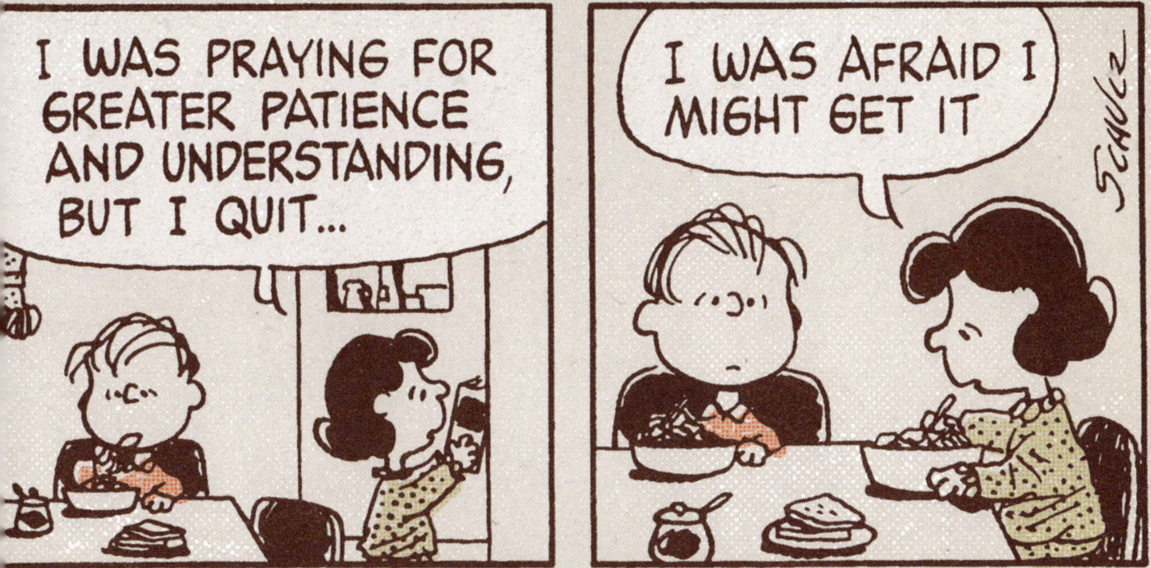

YOUR *love* HAS GIVEN ME *great joy.*

PHILEMON 1:7

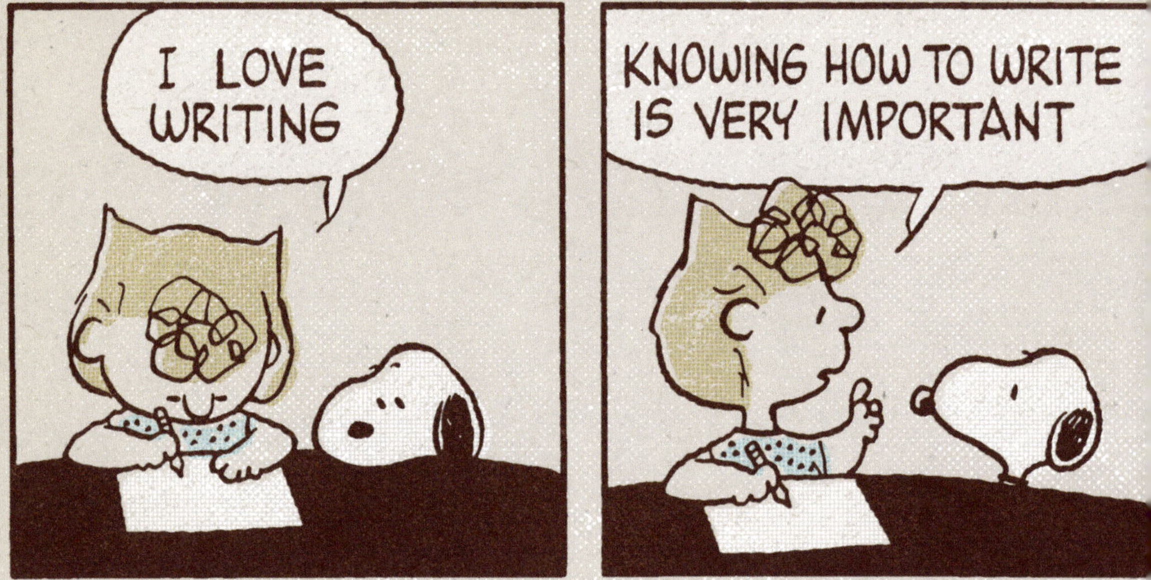
I LOVE WRITING
KNOWING HOW TO WRITE IS VERY IMPORTANT

IF WE *hope* FOR WHAT WE DO NOT YET HAVE, WE WAIT

FOR IT

patiently.

ROMANS 8:25

PEANUTS
WHERE HAVE YOU BEEN?
CHURCH SCHOOL.. WE'VE BEEN STUDYING THE LETTERS OF THE APOSTLE PAUL..
THAT SHOULD BE INTERESTING
IT IS..
Tm. Reg. U. S. Pat. Off.—All rights reserved
Copr. 1964 by United Feature Syndicate, Inc.
11-6

ALTHOUGH I MUST ADMIT IT MAKES ME FEEL A LITTLE GUILTY...
I ALWAYS FEEL LIKE I'M READING SOMEONE ELSE'S MAIL!
SCHULZ

SO YOU DON'T THINK JESUS EVER OWNED A DOG ?
NO, I DOUBT IT
© 1995 United Feature Syndicate, Inc.

BUT WHY?
IF HE HAD A DOG, ALL OF THE APOSTLES WOULD HAVE WANTED ONE..
5-29
SCHULZ

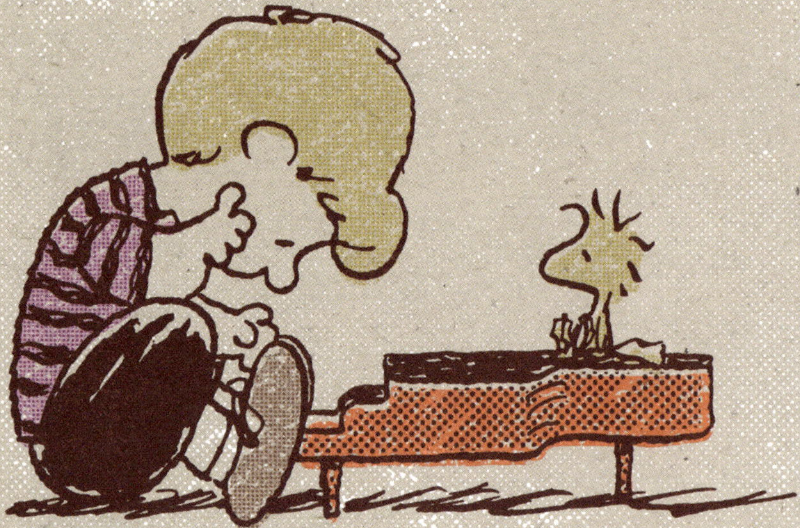

Peace BE WITH YOU.
LUKE 24:36

HAVE YOU SEEN MY BASEBALL GLOVE AROUND ANYWHERE?
© 1992 United Feature Syndicate, Inc.
"I KNOW NOT...AM I THE KEEPER OF MY BROTHER'S GLOVE?" GENESIS 4:9

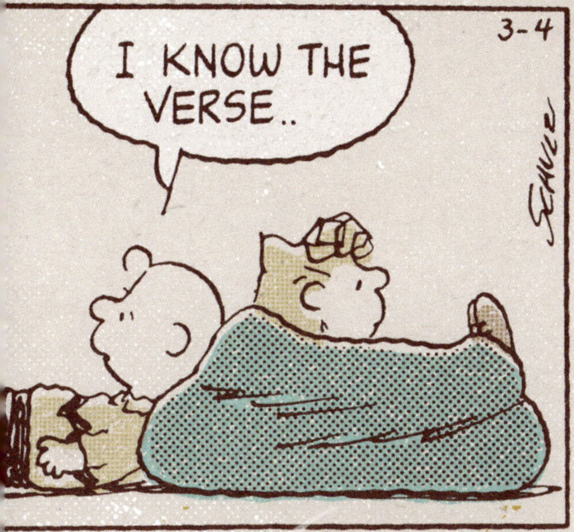
I KNOW THE VERSE..
3-4
SCHULZ

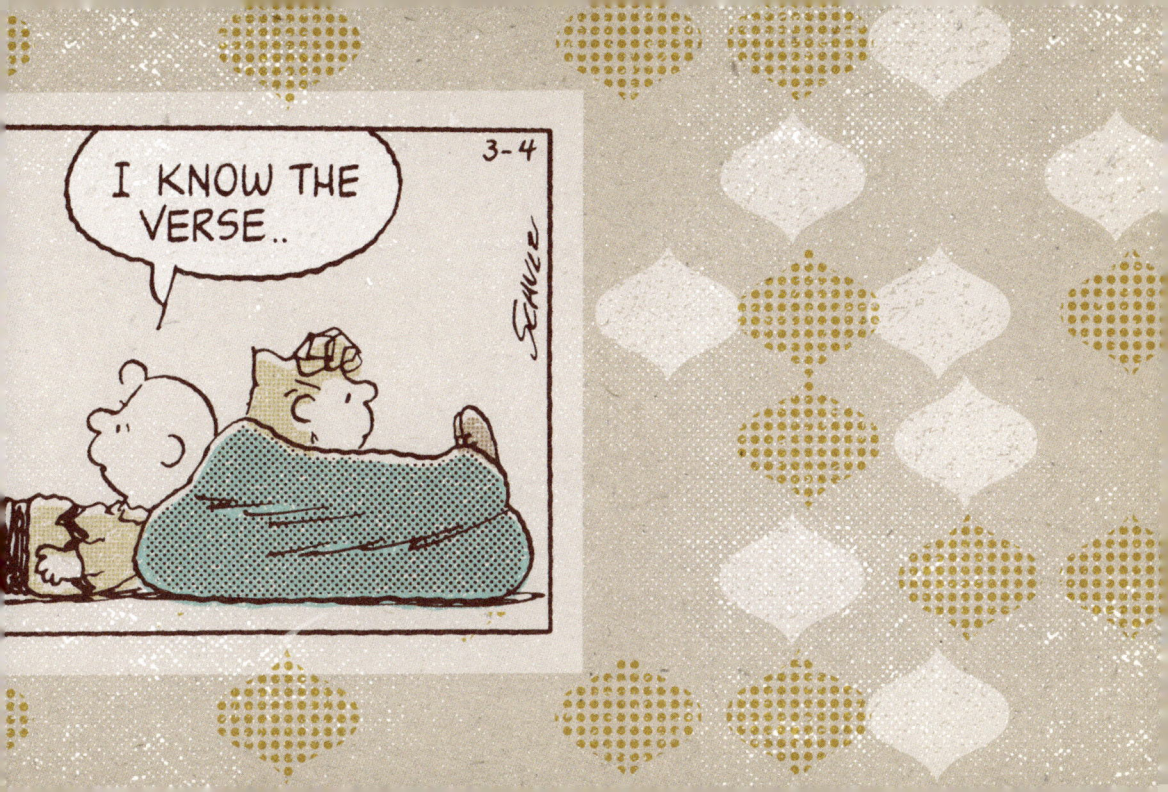

I DON'T THINK YOUR DOG IS OFFERING YOU ENOUGH COMPANIONSHIP!
HE'S SUPPOSED TO BE YOUR MOST FAITHFUL FRIEND..

IF NEED BE, HE'D EVEN GIVE UP HIS LIFE FOR YOU...
© 1988 United Feature Syndicate, Inc.
1-23
WAIT A MINUTE..
SCHULZ

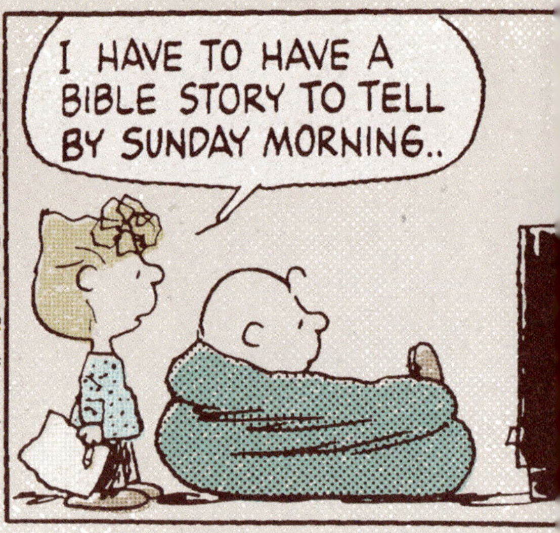
I HAVE TO HAVE A BIBLE STORY TO TELL BY SUNDAY MORNING..

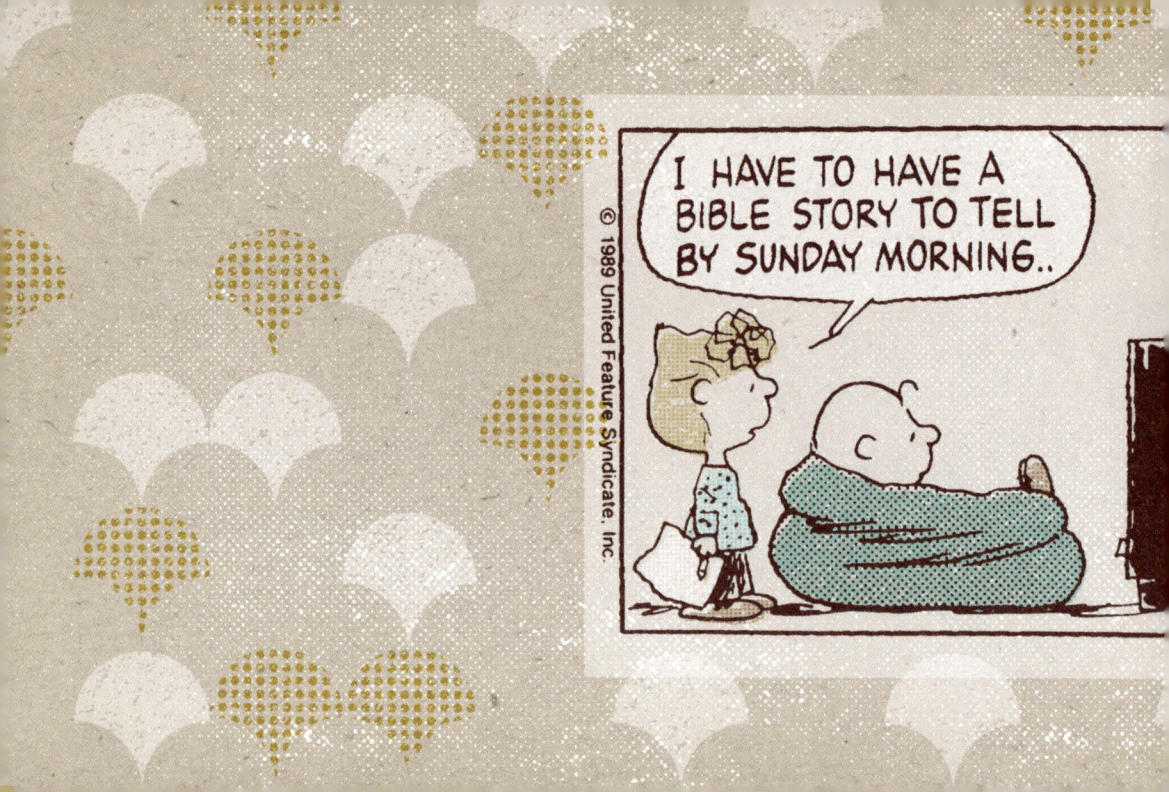

I WAS THINKING OF DANIEL IN THE 49ers' DEN..
LIONS' DEN
7-11
WHATEVER
SCHULZ

I HAVE NOT STOPPED GIVING *thanks* FOR *you.*

EPHESIANS 1:16

I FEEL GOOD.. I JUST GOT BACK FROM THE GROCERY STORE, AND GUESS WHAT...
THE OWNER AND HIS WIFE BOTH COMPLIMENTED ME.. THEY SAID I WAS A VERY NICE BOY...

IN THE SIXTH CHAPTER OF THE BOOK OF LUKE IT SAYS, "WOE TO YOU WHEN ALL MEN SPEAK WELL OF YOU.."
8-29
SO MUCH FOR FEELING GOOD..
SCHULZ
© 1987 United Feature Syndicate, Inc.

I WOULD HAVE MADE A GOOD EVANGELIST
YOU KNOW THAT KID WHO SITS BEHIND ME AT SCHOOL?
12-8

I CONVINCED HIM THAT MY RELIGION IS BETTER THAN HIS RELIGION
HOW'D YOU DO THAT?
I HIT HIM WITH MY LUNCH BOX!
SCHULZ

IF JESUS HAD OWNED A DOG, WHAT KIND DO YOU SUPPOSE IT WOULD HAVE BEEN?
I DON'T KNOW.. MAYBE A BORDER COLLIE..
I'LL BET THE DOG WOULD HAVE HAD A GOOD LIFE..
5-15

UNLESS HE GOT TIRED OF WALKING AROUND IN ALL THAT SAND..
SCHULZ

THE PLEASANTNESS OF A

FRIEND SPRINGS FROM THEIR *heartfelt advice.*

PROVERBS 27:9

MY REPORT TODAY IS ON KING DAVID
YOU KNOW WHERE KING DAVID WROTE HIS PSALMS? UNDER A PSALM TREE!
4-13
© 1978 United Feature Syndicate, Inc.

HA HA HA HA HA
I'LL BET DAVID WOULD HAVE THOUGHT IT WAS FUNNY
SCHULZ

DO THEY HAVE PRAYER IN YOUR SCHOOL?
8-31
© 1987 United Feature Syndicate, Inc.
NO, BUT LAST YEAR THEY HAD US OBSERVE A "MOMENT OF SILENCE"

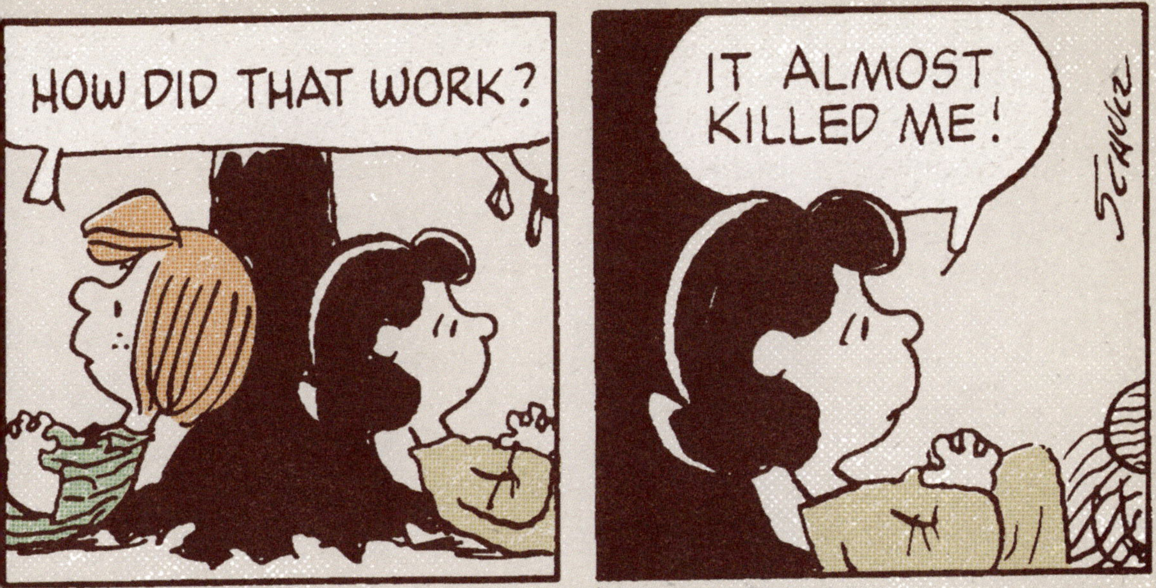
HOW DID THAT WORK?
IT ALMOST KILLED ME!
SCHULZ

PEANUTS
BOY, LOOK AT IT RAIN...WHAT IF IT FLOODS THE WHOLE WORLD?
4/13
IT WILL NEVER DO THAT...IN THE NINTH CHAPTER OF GENESIS, GOD PROMISED NOAH THAT WOULD NEVER HAPPEN AGAIN, AND THE SIGN OF THE PROMISE IS THE RAINBOW..

YOU'VE TAKEN A GREAT LOAD OFF MY MIND...
SOUND THEOLOGY HAS A WAY OF DOING THAT!
SCHULZ
Tm. Reg. U. S. Pat. Off.—All rights reserved © 1965 by United Feature Syndicate, Inc.

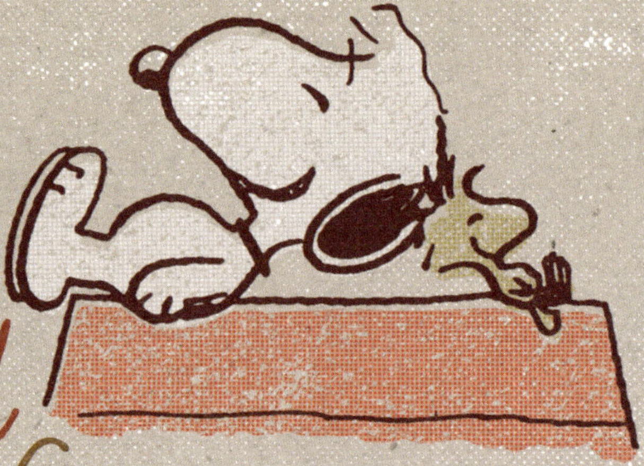

A *friend* LOVES AT ALL TIMES.

PROVERBS 17:17

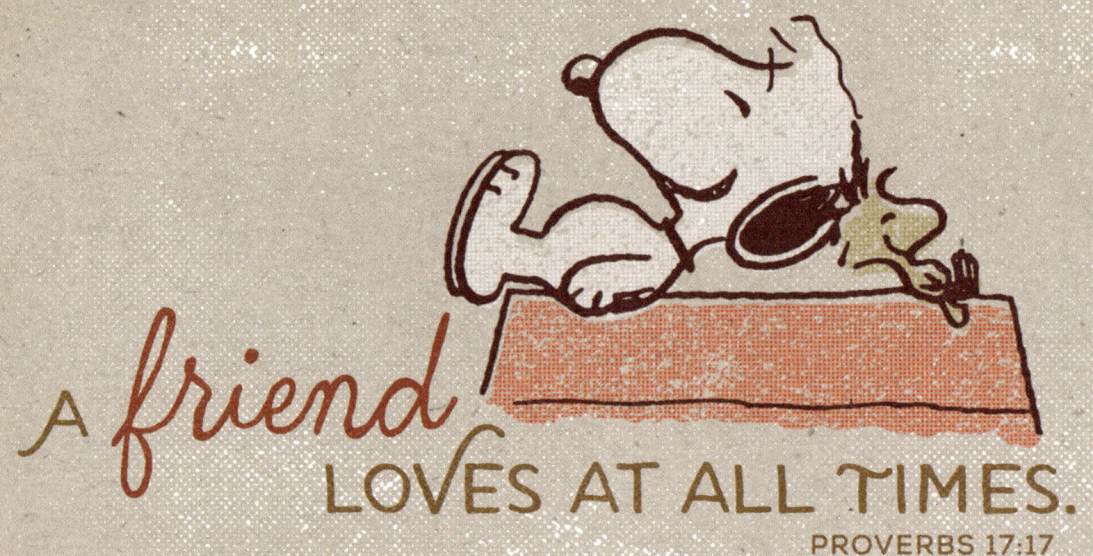

WELL, YES, MA'AM.. I GUESS WE COULD TRY... THANK YOU..
THEY WANT YOU AND ME TO TEACH AT BIBLE SCHOOL
TEACH WHO?

YOU MEAN THERE ARE PEOPLE AROUND WHO KNOW LESS THAN I DO?
SCHULZ
5-27

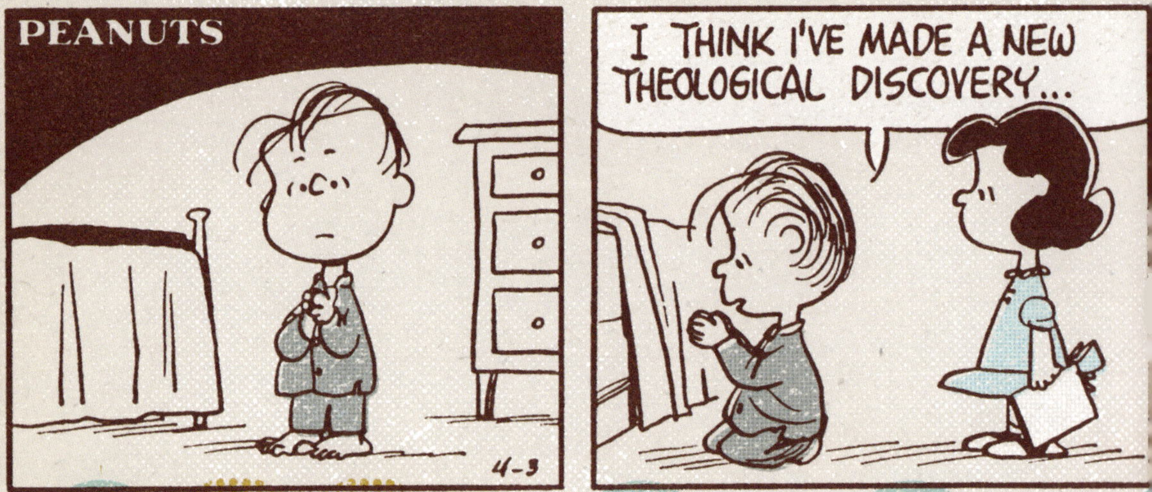
PEANUTS
4-3
I THINK I'VE MADE A NEW THEOLOGICAL DISCOVERY...

WHAT IS IT?
Tm. Reg. U. S. Pat. Off.—All rights reserved
© 1968 by United Feature Syndicate, Inc.
IF YOU HOLD YOUR HANDS UPSIDE DOWN, YOU GET THE OPPOSITE OF WHAT YOU PRAY FOR!
SCHULZ

YOU HAVE SHOWN

great kindness.

1 KINGS 3:6

PEANUTS
AND RIGHT AFTER CHURCH NEXT SUNDAY, WE'RE ALL GOING ON A PICNIC...
I DIDN'T KNOW YOUR FAMILY BELONGED TO A CHURCH..
3-30

SURE, DOESN'T YOURS?
Tm. Reg. U. S. Pat. Off.—All rights reserved ©1967 by United Feature Syndicate, Inc.
THEY USED TO...NOW THEY BELONG TO A COFFEE HOUSE!
SCHULZ

WHAT DID YOU THROW ME OUT FOR?!
MARCIE SAYS YOU WERE GETTING PAID TO BE MY TUTOR! YOU SHOULD HAVE BEEN DOING IT OUT OF THE GOODNESS OF YOUR HEART!
7-29

"THE LABORER IS WORTHY OF HIS HIRE" LUKE 10:4
HE'S QUOTING SCRIPTURE, SIR
IS THAT FAIR?
© 1986 United Feature Syndicate, Inc.
SCHULZ

Be happy...

AND LET YOUR *heart* GIVE YOU *joy.*

ECCLESIASTES 11:9

"I PLEDGE ALLEGIANCE TO THE FLAG OF THE UNITED STATES OF AMERICA AND TO THE REPUBLIC FOR WHICH IT STANDS,..."
"ONE NATION UNDER GOD, INDIVISIBLE, WITH LIBERTY AND JUSTICE FOR ALL"

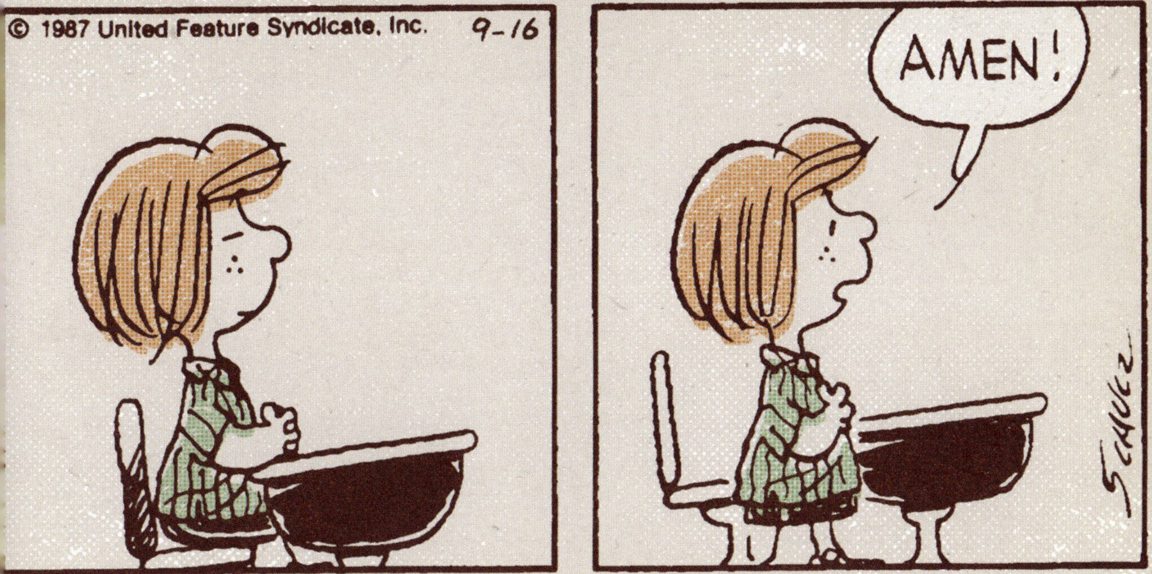
© 1987 United Feature Syndicate, Inc.
9-16
AMEN!
SCHULZ

If you enjoyed this book
or it has touched your life in some way,
we'd love to hear from you.

Please write a review at Hallmark.com,
e-mail us at booknotes@hallmark.com,
or send your comments to:

Hallmark Book Feedback
P.O. Box 419034
Mail Drop 100
Kansas City, MO 64141